AMERICAN ★ ★ ★ ICONS

The National Motto

IN GOD WE TRUST

Aaron Carr

LET'S READ
AV2 BY WEIGL
ADDED VALUE • AUDIO VISUAL

www.av2books.com

Go to **www.av2books.com,**
and enter this book's
unique code.

BOOK CODE

J137828

AV² by Weigl brings you media
enhanced books that support
active learning.

AV² provides enriched content that supplements and complements this book. Weigl's AV² books strive to create inspired learning and engage young minds in a total learning experience.

Your AV² Media Enhanced books come alive with...

 Audio
Listen to sections of
the book read aloud.

 Video
Watch informative
video clips.

 Embedded Weblinks
Gain additional information
for research.

 Try This!
Complete activities and
hands-on experiments.

 Key Words
Study vocabulary, and
complete a matching
word activity.

 Quizzes
Test your knowledge.

 Slide Show
View images and
captions, and prepare
a presentation.

... and much, much more!

Published by AV² by Weigl
350 5th Avenue, 59th Floor, New York, NY 10118
Websites: www.av2books.com   www.weigl.com

Library of Congress Control Number: 2013953030

ISBN 978-1-4896-0524-5 (hardcover)
ISBN 978-1-4896-0525-2 (softcover)
ISBN 978-1-4896-0526-9 (single-user eBook)
ISBN 978-1-4896-0527-6 (multiuser eBook)

Printed in the United States of America in North Mankato, Minnesota
1 2 3 4 5 6 7 8 9 0 17 16 15 14 13

122013
WEP301113

Every reasonable effort has been made to trace ownership and to obtain permission to reprint copyright material. The publishers would be pleased to have any errors or omissions brought to their attention so that they may be corrected in subsequent printings.

Weigl acknowledges Getty Images as the primary image supplier for this title.
Page 6: courtesy of www.coincommunity.com

Project Coordinator: Aaron Carr
Designer: Mandy Christiansen

2

CONTENTS

What Is the National Motto?

The national motto is a short saying that stands for the American people and their beliefs. The motto of the United States is "In God we trust."

IN GOD WE TRUST

5

A National Symbol

"In God we trust" was first printed on a two-cent coin in 1864. The motto has been printed on all American money made since 1957.

The First Motto

The United States once had a different motto. That motto was Latin for "out of many, one." This was because many groups of people came together to make the United States.

9

Asking for Change

In 1861, a reverend wrote a letter to Congress to ask for a change. He thought American coins should say something about God on them. Three years later, "In God We Trust" was first stamped on an American coin.

To Quote a Poem

The words "In God we trust" came from the poem "The Star-Spangled Banner." The fourth verse of the poem reads, "And this be our motto – 'In God is our trust.'"

Gone Missing

Some coins made in the 1800s and early 1900s did not have the motto on them. Many people asked Congress to make sure all new coins had the motto.

Back in Use

The motto has been printed on every penny made since 1909. It has been on every dime made since 1916. All American coins made since 1938 have had the motto in place.

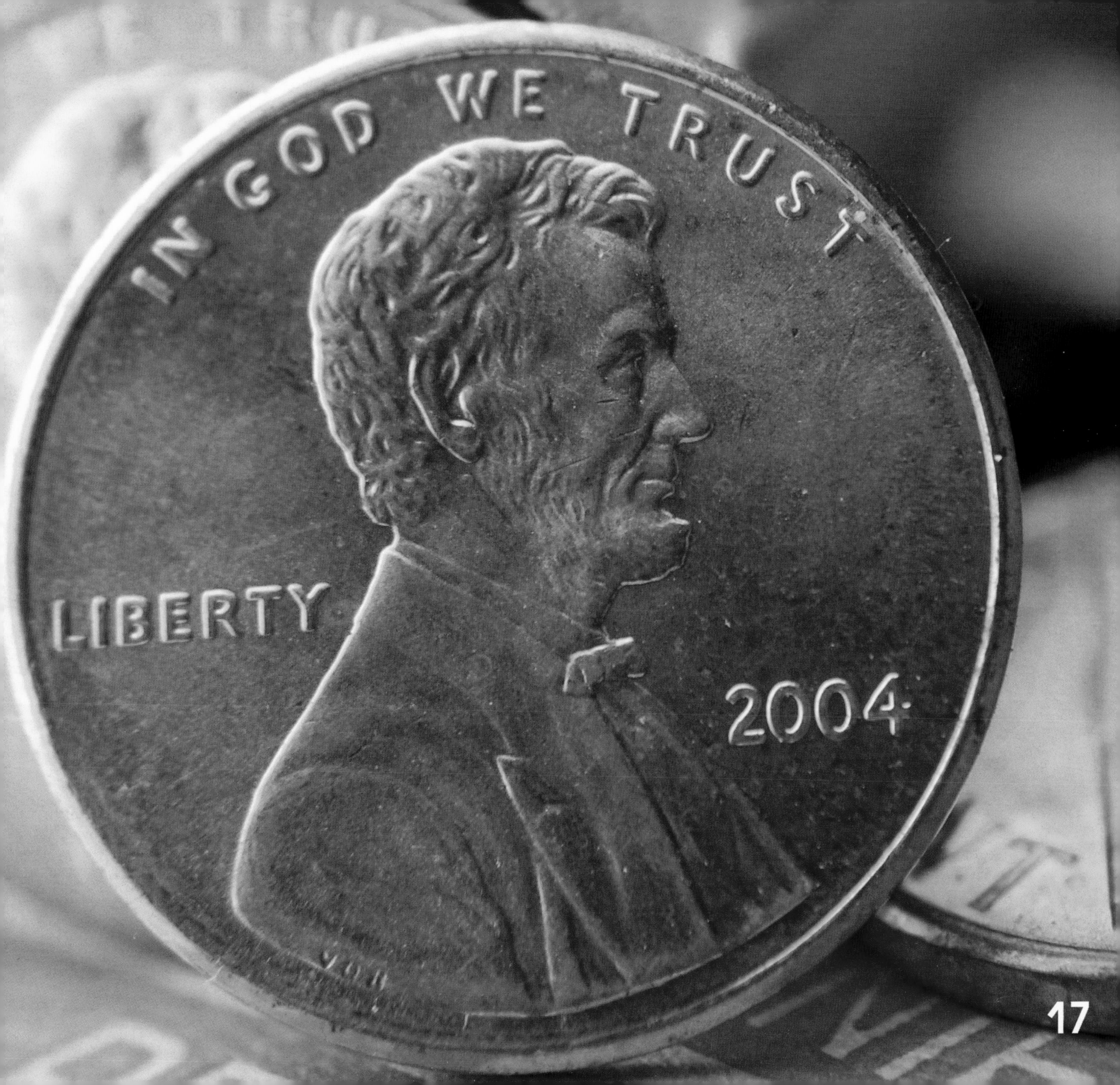
IN GOD WE TRUST
LIBERTY
2004

Becoming Law

"In God we trust" had been used for almost 100 years, but it was not made into a law. In 1956, the president made the motto part of the law. The next year, the motto was printed on paper money for the first time.

The National Motto Today

Today, "In God we trust" is printed on all coins and paper money in the United States. Some people have been asking Congress to change the motto. They went to court, but they lost. The motto has not changed since 1864.

21

NATIONAL MOTTO FACTS

These pages provide detailed information that expands on the interesting facts found in the book. These pages are intended to be used by adults to help young readers round out their knowledge of each national symbol featured in the *American Icons* series.

Pages 4–5

What Is the National Motto? A motto is a short statement meant to summarize the beliefs of a group of people. The United States motto is "In God we trust." This motto has been in use in the United States since the mid-1800s, but it did not become an official motto until nearly 100 years later.

Pages 6–7

A National Symbol The motto has been printed on American coins for more than 150 years. Since the first two-cent coin with "In God we trust" stamped on it was minted in 1864, the motto has been in continuous use. It has appeared on coins, on paper money printed since 1957, on license plates, and on government posters and other patriotic objects.

Pages 8–9

The First Motto The first motto of the United States was approved for use on the country's Great Seal in 1782. The motto, *E Pluribus Unum*, is Latin for "out of many, one." This is a reference to the original 13 colonies that joined to form the United States. This motto was also used on coins as early as 1795, when it appeared on the Half Eagle gold coin. In 1873, a law was passed stating that the motto had to be included on all U.S. coins.

Pages 10–11

Asking for Change In 1861, Reverend M.R. Watkinson of Pennsylvania wrote a letter to Secretary of the Treasury Salmon P. Chase. In the letter, Rev. Watkinson asked Chase to consider putting a reference to God on American coins. After reading this letter, Chase asked the director of the Philadelphia mint, James Pollock, to prepare a new motto.

Pages 12–13

To Quote a Poem The phrase "In God we trust" was inspired by a line from the poem "The Star-Spangled Banner." The fourth verse of the poem included the line, "And this be our motto – 'In God is our trust.'" The first verse of this poem later became the official national anthem of the United States. Salmon P. Chase originally thought to use "In God is our trust" as the motto but changed it to "In God we trust" in 1863.

Pages 14–15

Gone Missing In 1907, two types of gold coin were minted without the motto stamped on them. People were so upset about this that they complained about it to the government. Due to such strong demand, Congress passed a law in 1908 to ensure the motto would be included on future mintings of the coins.

Pages 16–17

Back in Use In 1938, a new Thomas Jefferson nickel was minted that included the motto. This was the first time since 1883 that the motto was included on the nickel. Before this, the motto was only used on a selection of coins, such as the two-cent coin as well as various gold and silver coins. After 1938, the motto was included with all new coins minted.

Pages 18–19

Becoming Law After nearly a century of widespread use, President Dwight D. Eisenhower signed a law making "In God we trust" the official motto of the United States. This law also stated that the motto must be printed on all American money, including paper bills. The first paper bills printed with the motto in place were minted the following year.

Pages 20–21

The National Motto Today "In God we trust" is the official motto of the United States, and it continues to appear on all forms of American money. However, the motto has come under attack in recent years. Some people think the motto should be changed to remove any reference to God. They believe religion should be separate from matters of government. In 2011, the Supreme Court rejected the case in favor of keeping the motto.

KEY WORDS

Research has shown that as much as 65 percent of all written material published in English is made up of 300 words. These 300 words cannot be taught using pictures or learned by sounding them out. They must be recognized by sight. This book contains 72 common sight words to help young readers improve their reading fluency and comprehension. This book also teaches young readers several important content words, such as nouns. These words are paired with pictures to aid in learning and improve understanding.

Page	Sight Words First Appearance
4	a, American, and, for, in, is, of, people, the, that, their, we, what
7	all, been, first, has, made, on, two, was
8	because, came, different, groups, had, make, many, once, one, out, this, to, together
11	about, an, change, he, later, letter, say, should, something, them, thought, three, years
12	be, from, our, reads, words
15	asked, did, have, new, not, some
16	back, every, it, place, use
19	almost, but, into, next, paper, part, time
20	they, went

Page	Content Words First Appearance
4	beliefs, God, national motto, saying, United States
7	cent, coin, money, symbol
8	Latin
11	Congress, reverend
12	poem, "The Star-Spangled Banner," verse
16	dime, penny
19	law, president
20	court

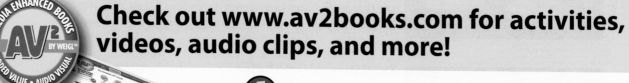
24